AFRICAN WRITERS SERIES

157

The Drummer in Our Time

The Drummer in Our Time

A. W. KAYPER-MENSAH

LONDON
HEINEMANN
NAIROBI · IBADAN · LUSAKA

Heinemann Educational Books Ltd
48 Charles Street, London WIX 8AH
PMB 5205 Ibadan · PO Box 45314 Nairobi
PO Box 3966 Lusaka
EDINBURGH MELBOURNE AUCKLAND TORONTO
HONG KONG SINGAPORE KUALA LUMPUR
NEW DELHI

ISBN O 435 90157 5

PR
9379.9
K3
D7

Set in Monotype Baskerville and
Printed in Great Britain by
Cox & Wyman Ltd, London, Fakenham and Reading

CONTENTS

The Blind Man from the North

Here, in the sun, by the hot and dusty way
Sits a man from the North gone blind.
In his hunger, he intones from an ancient lay
Of the ways of an Allah left behind.
But the crowd pass on, too dense to care or stay,
Too deaf to hear the news of the Allah left behind;
Yet he begs, and recites, and salutes the inner Allah
He believes is within each passer-by
For he sings of what he sees
Of a life of love and mercy
We should live in Allah's sight.

The Ghosts

Listen . . . it is evening in Kumasi,
And the lengthening sunlight fingers stroke the town
In a final caress, and move away westward,
Drawing a blind across the sky
Behind them as they move.
Can you hear the dark blind moving?
Listen!
Listen to the groaning noises,
Wild, nightmarish, fiendish wails . . .
Voices of the town dreaming,
Dreaming now at nine o'clock.
At Kejetia . . . the city's centre,
Bright new lights are on:
But here, where I stand,
In this deserted corner,

The lights are fading in our hearts,
And lovers have to part at sundown
If they want to meet tomorrow;
So let me go to Kejetia
To get a taxi home.
Cars will cross at Kejetia
If they dare not come near here.

They won't, or dare not come near here,
Because, from where you are,
You can hear
The offensive-defensive singing of a gang
And the clang and yell of slogans,
To keep their spirits up,
Or frighten attackers off.

Listen!
Did you hear it too?
The wailing of the pregnant woman
Caught under a crumbling wall blown up?
The children, terrified, and running away to safety
And the heavy clatter of the boots
Of a pair of racing policemen?

Did you count the explosions too?
Five, I think, in a rumbling sequence,
The last, the loudest of them all . . .
And five more homes will bleed!
I must run to Kejetsia,
To the mocking brightness at the centre
Of the pregnant town in labour,
To get a taxi home.

Kejetia was bare and quiet
Except for a lone figure . . . waiting . . .
Looking for a taxi home.
He moved away as I approached,
And would not speak to me.
His outstretched hand was thin and black,
And fluttered in the wind.
A passing taxi picked him up,
And picked me up too.
Then a curious pleasure flushed his face
To see me by his side.
We sat in silence for a while,
Then the driver spoke:
'I'll drop you, massa, at your gate,
And then . . .' 'Thank you,' I said.

[3]

'How long have you been in the town?'
My car companion asked.
'Six years,' I said, 'a long time.'
And he, 'Enough to know the joys
Of the town in days of peace and plenty.'
This, the driver did agree with;
(And I mourned that the town was ruined.
Ruined perhaps for ever).

Suddenly,
I seemed before an aged councillor.
For the weak old man
In a firm, wise voice
Spoke with the courage and the passion of a youth
In love with life
And said:
'Do you think that all is lost
Because your wailings reach high heaven
And your tidy, new-built mansions
Blown to bits overnight?
This is not a time for tears,
For mental failure or despair
Though opinion now is backed
By force that often knows no meaning
And any day,
Or so it seems,
Darkening clouds may break in blood
To flood the groaning city.
But this you can PREVENT and MUST!
By learning NOW to LOVE each other!

'This is not a time for jesting,

[4]

But for living as they did,
When our forebears had to save
The very ethos of the race.

'These are days when men must speak.
Shout the meaning of their souls
To the stone, the stool, the tree,
To the earth, the wall, the sky,
And the sun, when it appears,
But above all . . . to *Twedeampong*
Pointing to the blood of Abel
On the naked cement pavement!
You must speak to the heart that poured it.
And the evil hand that drew it.'

Suddenly there was a silence,
And I wondered where I was;
But it did not last for long,
For his voice rang out again.

'Listen . . . you whose youth is strong,
Human ways delay and sway,
Till they take a stable form
Like a lake on a bed of clay,
Supporting life, and giving beauty.
What you suffer in your day
Is the price you have to pay
As you try to come to rest
From the swaying force of change.

'You must learn what life can teach you:
And remember this, my son . . .

[5]

We have ruled ourselves before,
Though in a much more simple world.
And if your heart is sound and strong,
You may triumph where we faltered
And avoid the mocking pity
Of the man who, in his heart,
Curses and despises you.

'You deserve self-government now,
But you must avoid its dangers.'

At this stage, he pulled me to him,
And in a whisper, said to me:
'If you want to make it work,
Do not fall a prey to daily
Fear of death, and sudden death.

'Try, amid the blood and passion,
To discern a fitting answer
To the cry:
    "Self-governing what?
    Self-governing whom?"
And when an answer has been found,
With an inspiring present,
Worthy of your past and future,
And the genius of your blood,
You must leave the shifting sands
Of self-seeking and deceit
And erect far mightier mansions
On the rock of healthy souls.
Then . . . and only then, my son,
Will you sleep in peace at nightfall,

And the lovers will be gay,
For the lights at the heart of the city
Will illumine every heart
And destroy all enmity.'

We had reached the College gate
But the driver would not take
The fare I had to pay him.
Instead, I saw his face transfigured
As he smiled to my companion
Sitting in the taxi.
A chilly feeling made me shiver
Then as if I knew it all,
My companion said to me . . .
'He was once my private driver
When we shared your world.
He and I, and countless others
Look to you to save the day . . .
Some of what we left must die
But love and keep alive the best
And let that common love
Make you Friends.'

While he spoke, the taxi left;
And as I stood and shook with fear,
I saw two black and ghostly hands
Fluttering in the wind.

Man and Land in Africa

So much Sahara sunshine
Scorches man and land in Africa;
So many people scratch
A wounded soil to feel it dying
With a look that is their faces.

More of us are struck across
The eyes by senseless pain and want
Than those who take cool beer, and dance
Till midnight in a chrome and gold
Café fringed with coconut leaves;

Struck by savage hand of want,
Of ignorance in modern ways and thought,
Of killing illnesses and smouldering fear,
Of men thick-skinned enough
To fan the fear into a blazing fire
To cook a selfish pot of self-importance.

Life for most of us is painfully
The fate of one who tries in vain
Taking snuff on a windy beach.

We must heal the soil
To heal the soul, searching seeds
Of life to grow for daily bread;
Heal the soil that colonizing plants
May root and grow to stem
Advancing deserts turning farmlands
And our laughing homes into childless graveyards.
We must work for bigger money,
Money for whoever works;

[8]

For money is the seen harvest
Of long days of muscle labour,
Of our stretch of mind to find and use
Better ways of making more;
More to meet our pressing needs,
Buy a house, start a farm,
A firm, a press, an industry,
Buy a net, a plough, a car,
A chicken coop, a cow, a pig,
Build a willingness to venture,
To invest for still more money.

What we most desire
We must join and get;
What we live in fear of
We must join and fight;
What we deeply hate
We must all remove.
What we think unworthy
We must come together
Join and cast away.

My Group

Nothing is in small print,
Or written in a foreign tongue
To hide, preserve, protect.
You do not need a reading lens,
Or rare interpreters.

What is there to know
Is written large, plain
On blank, flat faces.

A repertoire of tricks
To earn a living,
Make the kids laugh,
The wife feel sat upon,
Then a beer among seasoned hands:
Afterwards, a snooze before the telly
When Karajan conducts,
Or a Celia decides.

Judgement is out of place;
For what is to be judged
Is not here, never meant to be.

Needs are simple.
Taste kept within the range
A village kitchen cupboard holds,
Protected from death or change
By instincts of a herd:
Its laughing whip, or shepherd's staff.

To depart in search of other
Ways of feeling, thinking, talking,
Is to walk away out of a moving train.

Who laid the tram lines
For this type of life?
Whoever did,
Now the passengers themselves
Protect the lines through beat country,
Keep them well away
From other districts of the human spirit,
Well within their bantustans.

The Trade and After

The hands that tore the sheets were Albert Schweitzer's;
hands that built a bridge to bring back Bach,
wrote the 'Quest' and built jungle huts
for mothers with their children near death.
They tore the thesis saying they were right
who tore the homes of Negroes for young slaves
and burnt an owner's trade mark in their backs.

It all seemed far beyond skyline of time,
but now and then a storm far up at sea
brings from groaning belly of a boat
cries of flesh bitten by sharp iron
and the crack of a whip on a salty bleeding back
of a stronger weakened man drugged with pain.

And strangers high, proud and bright as waves
breathe as healthy air the cry of death!

We turn the pages of their minds for clues
And find the vital chapters black with blood;

But when a dying baby laughs and lives
beside a mother praying in a hut
we bless the hands that tore the thesis up.

Lost Years

She spent her youth
learning how to cook
and knew a thousand dishes,
but the man she later married
ate only bread and milk.

Journeys through Cities

Lighted factories and office blocks
Are a feast of glass, glass holding light
Block by block on blocks of light
Rising solidly through the dark,
Up the sky, crystalline.
But we rarely think of it,
Meeting, passing in this light.

To the End

When winter came,
All that remained of these
Cool pools of shade beneath the trees
In Green Park and Hyde Park
Was thin black twisted lines
Of naked shivering nerves
Which suffered all but broke not;
And now, because they broke not,
Life has crowned the trees with sun-gay green
To cast cool shades again on heated brows
And nourish baby buds to smile
Into virgin flowers reaching for a kiss.

To Be

The Real is a deadly snake
That moves in a hollow garden.
It slinks unnoticed under grass,
Afraid, or just uncaring,
When, unaware, we pass it by
Unheeding, merely passing.
But to live it, is to tame it.
A tricky, risky job,
With death the cost of error,
And life the prize of triumph.

What can I tell you, Quester,
So keen to be alive?
This simple fact remember . . .
The risk is worth the taking.
Grip firm the head.
That's what to do.
The rest is only rope.
And to grip the head, and remove the fangs
Is the task you have to learn.
That knowledge is in this, my son,
That apart from God and evil,
The rest is mind and chemistry.

Well and Fearfully Made

We were not asked
For our opinion
When our skins were stripped of hair,
Showing to their best effect
Darling hills and diving valleys,
Scented meadows, gay-eyed flowers
In the soft grass of man's skin;

When our thumbs were freed and placed
For better grasping by our hands,
When our eyes were moved in front
For clearer stereoscopic vision
And our young breasts swelled to mimic
Our behind, our lips, a lusher
Copy; and our lobes of nerves became
Fine fingers feeling passing joys;

When channels of our feeding
Turned into a forward face
And the symbol of our need
Became a face-to-face embrace;

When electric flows of love outlighted
Candle lights they now replace,
And a round-the-year of appetite
Freed our roots from time and place.

We were not asked to pass the plans,

Not asked how economic or how best,
When a thousand biochemical systems
Building up in complex patterns

Streaming forces of our life
Then breaking down to free and clean them
Were designed, refined and made,

When their energy release
Gave my life and yours a name,
Our evolving push an aim.

Thanks to the unseen Hand
That bound my muscles,
Linked my bones,
Programmed me in chromosomes,
Then built a dam across my will
Letting out a pent-up power
That has helped me light my path
Through much darkness to great light.

The Happy and Free

We did not understand
quite why
the young boy wept
deprived of his friends.
But now we know.
The seeds of the happy
flower as the free!
And that which links
the boy's is stronger
far than our grown-up power
to understand.

Something of the same bond
unites the middle-aged . . . the
girls near the top
age-step, beyond which
is descent:
In their best age, and rage;
in motion, swiftest;
and in look fairest:
in build, strongest;
and in manner, sweetest:
in happy fling,
furthest, wildest now;
their smile
a waterfall baring
urgent energies of love,
stirring light about them
as they meet and make a
meaning in their free and
frank airs
in public places.

Such meanings are the pearls
of grace sought and treasured
by experienced tourists.

Yes on the Mountains

Up and down
the green-eyed mountains,
girls winnowing grains of beauty
have red hunger
in their tongues,
carefree joy
in their laughing thighs,
a soft, gay lift
in their ripe-wheat hair
and,
in their pure-blue-sky desire,
a white-cloud yes
that drifts to you
in their happy-welcome eyes.

Said the God in the Wind

Said the god in the wind:
'Your beliefs are insults to me.'

And the wind stood still
And our sacrificial smoke
Filled our eyes with tears.

Out of the wind spoke the god again:

'In mind, be men!
Stand up straight
And look on me,

'On my wounds and on my woe!
Why was I spat upon, reviled and killed?

'Because I condoned
                    Unreason and wrong?
Encouraged superstition,
                    Ignorance, and fear
Of the power of institutions
                    When dangerous to spirit,
Blocking man's way
                    Of movement to God?
Taking the name
                    Of the Lord in vain,
Making God serve
                    The will of men?

'The powerful would have left me alone, and gone
On living in wrong, as before I came.
Search the records and find out why,

'Since I came, it has not been the same:
Why they say I came to cast a
Cleansing fire on man's mind and altar.

'Your beliefs are insults to me.
Stand up straight
As men in my light,
And check your practices
And beliefs
Against my mind,
Against my heart.

'Rigorous reason there must be,
To bare the face of the facts I am
To correct and clean the inward parts
Of your live beliefs.'

The Tree in the Woods

From afar. our woods
Of church, of clan, of class
Look a solid mass of trees.
Only when you walk on grass
Among them is it known
That each tree stands alone.

Student Days

Amazing,
The sheer bulk,
The weight
Of junk,

Of priceless, rare antiques
In wood, silver,
Diamond, gold,
In various precious
Stones of song,
Which now are gifts
Of intellect and love which

Cambridge pushed
Our groping way,
In three short years!
Some twenty years ago.

How I Woke to Nature

Childhood pranks among the woods,
Whistling bird-song in the woods,
Looking up, deep in the woods,
Watching water in the woods;
Then the poets of the woods,
Wordsworth, Shakespeare, Shelley, Keats.
But there was a push quite early
At Mfantsipim one noon.
Reverend Warren picked me up
In his car that afternoon
When the green of the trees was new
In the rainy season sun.

Unobtrusively he said:
We are lucky with the green;
Cool on the eye: so fresh, so new.

I turned and looked. Felt the same.
Wondered with intense delight.
I kept the wonder safe with me
Till in time it became a key.

Thanks

To my homes, my family,
The eternal gratefulness of a tree
To the soil that helps it grow.
To my schools, and childhood friends,
The gratitude of a growing child
To the hand that feeds it daily.
To my enemies and critics,
Setting standards thought too high,
The 'thank you' sharpness of a cutlass
To the stone that sharpened it.

To my College on the Cam,
And on the highways of my world,
Praise of the eye to the sun, each dawn
That makes the darkness yield to light;
Praise of the tender climbing plant
To the tree that helped it up
Into sunlight and the sky.
To the state, and public bodies,
Vigour of the trumpet blower
Improvising great cadenzas
Praising him who bought the meal.

To my family of ghosts,
Friendly eyes that lacked pretence;
To Papa Ashon, Mame Efua Jane,
Undying love of a first-born son,
And to each, a gift of Edwen asa.

To my hidden life with the great,
In the Arts, and the Sciences,
And their treasured thoughts in books;
To my church, and private guardians,
The wonder and delight of a heart
Surprised by music of the ancient psalms
That has made me what I am.

Evaluation

From critical comment of the highest order
We ask for mathematical instruments
That measure the exact extent, the heights, the depth
Or how secure and sound emotion can
Be built upon the structures of our art.

We look for marks of meaning
In the muscle flexings of the aptest words
Alone or grouped for beauty and for power
Showing how the sensitive spirit gropes
To bare the greatness of the living act

And crowns our efforts with discoveries
That bring to consciousness
For the first time, perhaps,
The skin and marrow of reality,
The feel and fact of love
Thought, sought, lost or got.

Good critics take us round the galleries
Where we can know the secrets of creative act
On show; first hand and at source.

There we discover that works of Art,
Like science-goods and technical inventions,
Can light facets of the human mind
And are the proper witness to question
How man's skills can shift our aims higher
Without creating daunting, sheer despair;
Can kill complacency and free our strength
To push away impediments to love.

Differences

Before we map out differences
Of neighbours classed as races,
Let's trace the make, the inferences,
The attitudes that fixed the places
Each must occupy by law
By his choice, or by our claws.

Before we let loose wild horses
Over mines of 'not-alike',
Let the wise reveal what causes
Fears, cruelties or the strike
Against all unjust money-making
By the few who gun on, taking.

If we have to build our homes
On the land of 'not-alike'
Over which each child who roams
Is safe, on foot, or on a bike,
Let a team survey the land.
It may be rock, deep mud, or sand.

Every Perfection

For those whose minds
Are eyes of love,
Whose graces are faces
In gardens of love,

Every perfection is a sign
That there can be
A perfection of feeling:

Every purity, a sign
That there can be
A purity of being:

Every sweetness is a sign
That there can be
A sweetness of giving,
That is also the joy of living.

Freedom is Various

Copper beach leaves,
Grass, pine leaves,
Leaves of cactus,
Chestnut, rose leaves,

Desert, arctic, tropical leaves,
In and out of water leaves!

Think on it!
What shapes, what colours,
Sizes, textures,
Thin, light; leathery, thick:

Serving in their healthy fitness,
In their rightness
To their world
Life of their particular trees!

These, in their variety
Are what our freedom is:
That each may find a way to be;
Where, or what we have to be.

Precious

In sea waves, and leaves,
In flowers, and pure white
Clouds of snow on mountains,
Nature that receives as delight
Our gifts of architecture, fountains
Man's hopes, man's beliefs
Up the face of heaven in the sun
In how her background seasons turn, her waters run –
Though man need not be there to see or care.

We stir with joy at gull flight
Over blue seas; at the birch tree in evening light.

But the presence
        Of a well made girl
And a boy's reachings, tell
        In a whirl
Of daylight delight
        How men and women light
The face of nature
        With their being there, their gesture!
And are by far the most precious,
                most delicious
Beings we can see and touch,
Communing and creating
Through sex and sensibility;
Matching fitting architecture
With their grace, their culture
Felt as form or gay civility.

Whenever human beings meteor
Bright among their architecture,
Or among the shades of Nature,
Pleasure turns a pearl to treasure
A smile on the moving lips of Nature

Trusted Freedom in Love

'Benyin dze wommfa n' nnsi tam ano'
     (You do not tie a man at the end of your cloth
     to keep as you do with coins)

Do not knot him in your waist-
Cloth, to keep him safe.
     He won't be in
Although his body's in,
     He will follow taste
And wander through the television worlds
     Parading their girls.

You will keep him,
     If you lose him
To his will you should trust, which will
     Not stay or stray
Unfaithfully away.

     If you trust him,
You will see him
     Come back home
With a pile of coal-
     Fire from his roaming:
Glowing fire for your winter coal.

Small Price

It is the same, every working morning.
The laboratory tables fill with racks of test-tubes
Full of specimens of blood; or trays
Of slides smeared for a corpuscle count.
On other tables, and in groups,
Are row on row of carefully labelled
Bottles of stool, urine, sputum
From known patients; or suspected cases
Waiting anxiously for the first verdict
Of the crucial search, the chemical detection;
A verdict that at once can turn their sun dark,
Eclipsed at noon, or else set them free
From temporary captivity to fly away again.

The laboratory assistants set to work,
Confident, skilled, thorough to a fault;
Knowing what it takes
To handle messengers of death,
Or face revulsions of their own emotions
At the sight of slime,
The stench of faeces
And contagious urine.

These, for them, do not deter,
For they have learnt to work with care.
Besides, their search begins beyond
The repellent stench, the slime, the risks;
For chemicals there are that can destroy them,
That the search may safely start beyond their power.

Soon, by tried colour-tests or heat,
By chemical reactions with reagents,

Observing sediments, behaviour, strength,
And by a thorough microscopic search,
The outlines stand out clear and firm
For a 'yes' or 'no' to this, or that
Suspicion, or unlooked-for tragic surprise.

But why go poking human mud,
Human slime, and liquid waste?

Because in these are kept recorded
Histories of what the body
Has allowed as guests, gone fatal;
What germs have fed and bred in vital
Organs; whether, and how far the body
Was a prey to their clever, cruel ways.

However much their feel or smell
Repel us, we go to them for what they have
To tell us, help us do. For stool,
Blood, urine, sputum are such
Vital witnesses readily available
To answer the questions we must ask
To get to the looked-for truth in the body;
Truth to guide our skill to heal and save,
That we must get beyond what obstacles
They put before us,
Push their unlocked doors and keep them open
For what they can give.
What the feeling does not like, or the senses shun,
Is a very small price indeed to pay;
Especially where we need not run away!

At work, what may repel is
Like the unfamiliar, to the fastidious guest;
Or the social scientist, in field research,
Away in another land, another tribe;
Who must expect, ignore, or neutralize
Habits that may jar, or even threaten
Him, but once contained, can set him free
To search the life of another social river,
To scoop and sieve its diamonds from its mud.

Destroy the Hatred
between the Races

Destroy the hatred;
Not the man:
Unless the two
Are one.

Uproot this crime
Twixt man and man;
And cast it
In the sun.

That it may never root again,
Burn it all, and if you can,
Forget the harm it
Has done.

Too Late

Jaded, doped, desensitized,
Her nerve-ends,
                  blunt with corns,
Exposed too soon to shocks
Of rough use tramping stony
Paths of dirt and thorns:
              Or turned aggressive horns,

She hurls herself with scorn
At life demanding men
With Lesbian skill to wake
What she had killed, and to take
Her back as innocence again.

These Sour

These sour my taste,
Break my back,
Bend my mind,
Throw me into knotted loops
In a maze without direction.

I would you did not tell me
I was other than my friends,
That the normal do not sit
In silence listening to Bach
Or to talks by old professors,
Scientists, economists,
Priests, painters, poets.

Then I would not have
Had to go, a dog
Sniffing round the stranger's gifts,
For proof that you were right,
That the best is bad for me,
That I must be what I am, no more:
Be other, lower, than my friends,
Only to pretend, hereafter,
With no proof to show for it,
That the busy world must stop
In silence, while I tell
How great I am.

The Poet Farmer

Initiate, newcomer,
Poet 1970;

What grey rails
vanish in the mists
up heights of age,

bringing you where
a Greek woke at dawn;
sat at breakfast:
   What for breakfast?
Spoke to servants,
   What about? a wish? a gossip?
prayed to God
of the light of the intellect;
prayed for the peace
and the fine, untearing strength
of the civilized intelligence;
prayed that each may share in all
that the love of life may live;

then, set down his thoughts
in order, in the dance
of birds, of waves, of leaves
or of rising flames of beauty;

or, where a prophet
poet, Roman
in oration, lordly, civil,
greeting in his dress
our Kente,
taught in verse a love of law.

Do not let me hear
of the fear of the barnacle neighbour.
None would know how safe the road
if we spent our days at home;
never wandered; never met
travellers from a distant land.
As the only farm you know
is the plot behind your hut;
as you never venture far
to inspect a neighbour's farm,
how can you, in conscience, boast
of your farming skill and name
lacking standards to compare with,
or the means to prove your claim?

The Price of a Name

A bed, clean, warm, well made
For a winter lonely night,
And a kindly face or two,
That is all I needed here
In this city.
What a pity
That I pay now seven times
For a hard night here in this hotel
With a paper front for face.

You have paid for a name. Name?
Yes, all of us do.
Mention any famous name,
Say he said so and so,
So and so on art, on love,
Politics and kicks of drug,
On the pill, or the striving will,
And at once we rise to inhale,
Dazed in a name's incense, buying
Any trash at any price.

An Egg

```
        you grasp
      too hard. You
  C   R   U   S   H
  when    you    should
  see      in      me
    an           egg
    for         tender
      s t e a d y
          hands
```

Kariba
[*conversation with a tourist*]

Kariba, Kariba,
Damn your Kariba!
Your roaring wheels
Drowning the laughter of the roaming jackass,
Silencing song of forest birds,
Grunts, howls and yelps of hippos,
Blackening skies of virgin sounds
Till the lion's rainbow roar
Disappears in one dull black.

Damn Kariba for these crimes
We have meted to the beasts,
Those poor dears, those darling dumb
Driven wild in drowning floods.

But what say you of the men around
There, women, children struggling to make
Good, lacking means to raise their standard
To the height of foreign friends?

Black men are not my concern,
Let them see how they survive.

But the helpless poor dear ones,
Angels of the woods and waters,
Why destroy them with a dam?

Have You Read them All?

But,
have you read them all,
all these books?
Isn't it appalling?

Well!
I like the scorn
in your voice
like lethal toys
out of control,
a knife in wicked hands
cutting up my net
spread out to dry.

But
scorn is furthest from
the way I feel towards
these books . . . my various lines
of life, baited with a finding love
for a catch of other lives.

You
have your lines too
(we all have)
leading into other lives
along which love may travel
either way, though many lines
may tear and lie flapping
unconnected, dead, unused.

[45]

Yours
may be very much like
what your baby needed in the womb,
sightless, unreflecting,
cushioned in a dark
isolation.
If so,
you are not really free
from the need of what
is kept in books.

I happen to require
eloquent, reflecting lines,
good-conducting, bringing in
at various pressures light,
sound, heat, to touch, move, delight;
strong lines which pull ashore
a singing net of many fishes
for my outstretched hands, my hungry looks
in my row on row of books.

Perhaps Hereafter

Perhaps hereafter
Suddenly alone although in company,
Time will stop for you;
And you will hear again my voice,
Not because of what I said
But of what I was, and how.

May you feel, however briefly
In your fine imagination
Glad caresses of a river,
And a sea's receding waves.

The Dangers

Three wild lions
with the look of sheep
stalk the skipping lamb of marriage:

Hungry need
is one of them:
for the long married,
so they say,
need love-making
all around them,
hungry men prowling daily
dying over them;

and a wife,
yes, every wife
sometime married
dreaming wicked
longs for varied shocks
of pleasure red blood gay, as dancing hey!
not the same
grey, stale
surprise;

and to feel all served, for use,
available
where needed most
is a right . . .
the bright red glow
of dawning hope
of each woman
seeking love
from the sudden highway neighbour.

Stale taste
comes next;
the neither hot
nor cold look,
the burnt ash
of the flaming wood
that is all that may remain
of a wedding, years ago
that was only dress and starch:
the touch that jerks
as if a blow
confused at cross-roads
where to go,
till taking bed and board
for granted,
bed and board
shore us up, bored,
broken, on a beach
deserted, lonely, out of reach.

Last, the deadliest
of them all . . .
the look, the laugh, the chance remark
that stirs an ancient, stinking pool,
the simple act with a history
of warring wills and muddy ways,
the grunt that pulls a wild nettle
right across a smiling face
leaving only voiceless gestures
of a puzzled, pained gape!

These three,
roar and jump
from a stranger's blood-shot eyes
wild with a dirty killer's rape.

Dust Will Survive Us

Earth loosely clothed in leaves:
Is rock beneath whose layers show
Its grip, as its eager hand receives
Returning substances which grow
To fall on it, like one who grieves,
Too blind with tears to know
He falls to decay. Dark earth retrieves
The dying autumn glow
For show in a returning spring
When, again, the song birds sing.

Its dust will survive us: the soil we dig,
Throw about, or build
With, trample under foot, or stick
A pole in, to see it skilled
In calling into life the outcast sick.
The earth we heaped and filled
A grave with, burnt into jug, into brick,
Will take us back as silt
Which, but for the harvest of our mind,
Is all we leave behind.

Sweet Age

It is because
the soul's honey
like great psalms
or well loved music
tastes better, longer far
than the solid breakfast honey
melting on the hungry tongue
that ripe age
compels and draws us
after it, for satisfaction

He Has Learnt the Different Ways

He had learnt
the different ways
to destroy the sudden flame
that may show up, or reveal
his proud face as masking shame.

That must never,
never happen.
Anything else, but exposure.
Nothing must disturb composure
he has toiled by fraud
and cleverness to build
till he can pass
as a man of rank . . . a lord;

till you feel him
as a shoe
walking on your fallen face.

So he acts, a murderer
to the nearest flame of merit:

For the flame of match or candle,
puff of firm, steady air
blown upon it till it's out.
For the flaming wood or cloth,
just a dip in deep cold water.
For electric bulb and torch
just a turning of a switch.

For a roaring petrol flame,
flame of forest, house or town
chemical extinguisher
or his city's fire brigade:

but the outcome is the same;
match the method to the kind;
to the type, the size of flame
till there is no awkward light
to reveal his need as shame.

Then when darkness fills our world
out will ring his proud voice
like an actor on the stage
full of wild gesticulations
or like a soldier who has drunk
strong, dry wine of brutal death
making us a cornered audience
in our bright midday made blind;
with his knocks of rude 'look!'
each a lash on helpless eyes
by a nervous, blinking star.

No

A thin dark curtain of one night
Is all there is between me and the
Foul horrors from the steaming rot
Of superstition and disease;
Below the fresh hygienic consciousness
Your world expects, but you reject—
You who have whole centuries
Of thick black blocks of concrete
Night between you and the horrors.

So seek some other would be dancer
Who will dance your beat, and rock
To your anarchic morals.
'Because I do not hope to turn . . .'

Mirror of Terror

Order
Is a corpse's bones
Picked clean in chemicals,
Laid in place,
Loosely linked:

And in its icy, desert waste,
A little wind
Of unexpected passion
Is enough to stir
A ghostly terror all about us,
Lifting up the skeleton
In a white macabre dance
Through the churning dusk,
    Confusion.

Order out there,
Is a dress of many feathers
Each a gift from a passing bird
Which, any day,
When cold wind blows
Will come to take its gift away
Till, one by one,
The feather-dress
Scatters unconnected
With our need
In freezing rain.

Unless the order
We have made
Is mirror of an inner order,
Harmony is not in us:

And the rise and break of our feelings
Find no patterning
To discipline or inner beauty
Or to deeper meanings;

And what we lack
May help a stranger put
A mask . . . a devil's, or a tyrant's
On the order we have made
Till our mirror
Turns a terror . . .
Makes the neatly folded linen
Or the latest on the table,
The dirty plates and underwear
Washed in Pril or Daz or Omo
Easy traps of false alarm;

Books, glass, polished wood
Arranged, or stored to keep their shine
Mere slippery slopes for a child's feet,

And bright-eyed borders of a Persian
Carpet, cleaned, stretched straight,
Inspect our glad in-coming shoes
Only for the dirt they bring.

[56]

Such tiresome order
With a mask
Becomes polished teeth of death,
Or bright electrocuting chairs,
Rust-resisting, waiting,
Like a hangman's noose
Dangling round our face, our neck,
Ready for the stretch of death
At the turning of a switch.

Sufficient unto the Day

First, the moral *rubbish*, heaping
high at our doors of knowledge;

then the dark hosts of *locusts*
coming south across our hearts,
turning sun to source of darkness,
leaving fields of richest clothes
as useless lines of flapping rags;

and now, it is a dark *rain*
falling blindly on our heads
shaking us with fears, and tears
freezing on our lined faces.

I Blamed Them Once

I blamed them once,
the red dust stupor
rising underfoot;
the sun-baked bed
of the paper-dry lake.

I blamed them once,
the barren, and the thorny;
the rag in the storm, rust in mud;
the broken nail, and the log, worm eaten.

Why, I wondered,
why no rise of voice, or fist
in the face of the gentleman sky
while the dust storms rose as blindness
underneath the midday sun?

I blamed them once,
but now, no more;
for I too did not care enough;
not enough to write and cry out
wound-raw wild, as a sick, weak child
hurt by boiling oil poured
across his legs, thighs and trunk which
seared its skin till it could not breathe.

No; my silence is as dumb
as the numb, accepting gape
raised to meet a master's face . . .
the gape of dry mud split in the sun!

Can I sit and dine with the young men
in whose conscience songs of protest
formed against the wars of Spain
or whatever fashionable
dress oppression courted men in,
those young men who spoke and died
with their bellies full of fire?

How many fires are lit and spread
by a cocktail of my poems?
How many songs, conceived, are still-born?
How many of the few, alive,
huddle close with face of stone
in a pavement through the shopping
centre where the few alone
can enter by the bullet-laws
of guns, and the barbed whips of spite;

where the many, turned pavement,
watching passing muddy heels
stepping insults down their souls
heat with pain, but can't complain?

Suppose

'Suppose. Let us suppose!'

That is how it all began.
That is how it does begin.

That is where our laws were born,
Why philosophers were crowned.

That is how the lines were drawn,
How the high barbed-wired walls
Rose to keep our race divided.

So simple, straight on, logical
From that step a thousand miles.

Would that when we say 'suppose'
We would see from root to rose.

The Drummer in Our Time

Drummer, heartbeat of our being,
When you drum our ancient bravery
Do not miss our present history:

Of Kweku Ananse's modern children
Sent to trade and bring home profit
Taking with them gifts and greetings
To the rivers of the world,

The Thames, Rhine, Mississippi, Tiber,
Jordan, Seine, St Lawrence, Volga;

And the bundles they returned with
Some of seeds and some of iron,
Some of stirrings of the spirit,
Gifts of standing in the presence
Of a beauty fierce and holy;
And departing, touched, on fire;
Gifts of tongue, of skills, of vision:
Gifts of wild creative anger:
Gifts of signposts out of danger:
Gifts of patient, faceless effort,
Disciplined, informed and fruitful.

May your drumming, music, meaning
Turn our heads to look about us
At the boys who swing on cranes,
Plant the new seeds in the fields,
Feel a growth with growing plants,
Move the earth or build the village,
Ride the seas, fly our planes,
Mend equipment, tend machine

[62]

At the factories; at the dam:
Civil servants (firm bridges),
Politicians and professors
Scientists in overalls
In laboratories, and schools;
Girls skilled to their finger tips
In saloons, in wards, hotels,
All working for themselves
By themselves, like the market women,
Pausing to recall a proverb
In that high-life hit, reflecting
And creating newer proverbs
With the poem of their effort—
For the drummer of tomorrow.

May your drumming still our noise
For the girl that sings a seed,
Flowering beauty in our lives,
Making Ghana fairer, better;
And each child, a proud ancestor.

Four Hours a Day

Boredom and inaction come as twins
With murder in their turgid arms and eyes.

What has kept their slaughter from our paths
Is vigilance, discipline, and planning;
Not forgetting simple sacrifices . . .
This beer money for that paperback;
Or a strictly kept routine, four hours a day
Spent in pleasures free from money making
That a meditative Amo on odurja
Hand in hand with a Bach may spread a mood
Of deepening contemplation on our thoughts,
Lead them through a world of revealing mirrors,
Hold in check stampeding, warring passions,
Chain them to some strong silk-cotton tree
Of an aesthetic principle that guides
Our energies into acts meaning love. . . .

Four hours could be peg enough
To hang attention on, and keep it there
Concentrated on some passioned search . . .
Some chosen form of life not far to find,
Some score of flowers in the neighbourhood,
A dozen birds, butterflies, beetles.
Some life in pool, or river, or on a shore,
In great cathedral forests or in grass,
Some microscopic beauty magnified
To find the ways the webs of life are woven,
How the parts fit to puzzle death:
Some mineral or rock or shower of stars
Showing earth as lonely, in bright company;
To find how so much beauty is deployed,

[64]

Renewed to serve today, and life tomorrow.

Another time, a book may fill our world
Splashing us with pleasure
In the waves of a day's heat;
Filling memory with sounds of thunder
And a baby's laughter,
Bringing us a feel of lively grasp,
As men's spirits stretch to match their knowledge
In science, in politics, in culture;
And children roam a garden picking fruits
From high religion and our modern faiths.

When the time is ripe, I flex my muscles
Digging, planting, watering, manuring,
Watching seedlings break the loosened earth
Like splitting egg-shells letting out their life.
Soon when frail and tender leaves open
I watch with wonder how the dangling life
Accommodates the tearing force of wind
And falling missile-drops of rain, turning both,
In time, to stirring music for a dance.

Then there is the coming of the buds
Rising skyward in a dull hood
But bursting into fireworks of flowers—
A coloured brightness in a night sky.

At night, to rest the limbs and share my life
In gratitude with her who pokes its fires,
Smoothes its pillows, mends its torn clothes
And lies awake when pain drowns my sleep,

[65]

We put a record on the gramophone
And for a while we hear the language
Of a soul surprised by love,
By a beauty's purity – a child's eyes:
A joy joins our souls to their source
In music of a Telemann or Bach,
And we feel our roots fed,
By Beethoven and his friends.
Other records bring us other gifts,
Readings by professionals of plays,
Of poetry of radio sketches and of passages
From bible and prose of diamond beauty
Cutting clean, as diamonds do,
The filth of life away.

Sometimes drums may summon us
Out to see a chief pass, gold and shining,
Rich in right to rule, in retinue.
Or we may attend a chief's court
To hear a linguist spread in royal language
A peacock tail of tribal history, lores,
Proverbs, edicts, ancient wisdom—
Pillars of a people with a proud past
And a prouder future:

Future with its traffic signs pointing
To a Legon landmark or a Kwaabotwe
To teeming sites of dams and factories
Of self-help project in a humble village,
To the latest exhibitions of art,
Of fashion shows, furniture and crafts,
Of harvest of Science and technology,

[66]

In Trade Fairs where nations show their wares
To kindle public want for skills and knowledge:
To films, plays, concerts, poetry readings,
Public entertainments – public schools
For the young, and the active not-so-young alike:
To training grounds of games on land or water.

Like homing birds from a storm,
Friends may drop in for a chat—
Our best chance for talking shop
And listening to any, bringing light
Into the darkening hall where we
Just sit and talk.
For me the talking stops when suddenly

A dancing tune begins in something heard or seen
Or touched; and words, a few at first perhaps,
Rain on my nerves; and something in me
Orders them into a breathing, sweating form
Dancing to a deeper music for the inner ear.

Preparing the Ground

Too much sunlight.
  Draw the blind.

Too much street noise.
  Shut the window.

It's too windy.
  Close the door.

But here, in sunny Africa,
Can a privileged few for ever keep
A strong, happy world away;
Its light, laughter, fresher air,
From the shadows of their lounge
And keep, untouched, the status quo,
With the hoary, broken, thinning cry

'B – because they must b – be chairs to sit on;
Living fossils for our mirth;
Or large pools of good cheap labour;

B – because they must b – be where they are,
Let us keep the colour b – bar?

A Thorn against My Face

Your looks are thorns,
Bruising, till I bleed.
But you are nice
With a wry smile.

Behind your eyes,
Buried in your smile,
Your sight is better.

Helter skelter run
The natives, naked,
Wild, diseased, and dirty;
Jumping, kicking dust around
Lacking discipline, or order;
Sly, lazy, slimy, brutish;
Thanks to the 'children's stories'
And the television tales.

Pity, I am here; so near.

You are scornful
That my looks should shine
Like money newly minted;
Cleaner, quieter and saner
Than the types that romp around
In the nursed imagination.

But perhaps I should be glad
That you do not rise to kick me
With a foul shout that you wish to clean
What, around, is your world.

[69]

In another, stranger country,
You would act, and not just look,
Act the law to sweep me off
Into dustbins of contempt.

Excuse my writing in this vein
But
Time we spoke more quietly, plainly
Gave a meaning, hearing; clearly.
Time the louder voices ceased
And our choking tensions eased.

If I Turned

BLACK:
If I turned white, quite white,
what would you, in anger, miss?

If you turned white, quite white,
healthy with the fire of snow,
kept your open welcome face,
lived not as a cliff or cactus;
living with, and not against,
seeing in the passing neighbour
brother's, or a sister's needs;
if you kept undimmed your love
for the wider joy of all,
not forgetting nearer needs,
it won't matter in the least
if your change permits a feast
once a while where all are friends,
in participation high life
on deep lively lakes of meaning.

WHITE:
If I turned black, quite black,
what would you, in anger, miss?

If you turned black, quite black,
earned the riches of the dark,
and kept your spirit; stayed alive;
kept your stirred intellect,
laughter-loving, quick eyed, fine;
kept a clean drain of reason
and the habits of your world,
its skills, maturities, and order;

being sunlight in bad weather;
playing, ripe in autumn sun,
turning on each touch of love
sensitive as litmus paper
to the acid change about you
in the medium of your life,
spoken to by wordless music;
if you kept all this unchanged
underneath your changed skin
it won't matter in the least
what new colour you become.
I would seek what could emerge
from your black, which white may miss.

Participation
[*In the children's world*]

Children at play clap one another
Dancing: clasp each other
Leaping, cheering the other.

Children at school cheer one another
Miming: join one another
Singing; learning together.

Their living is a making game,
Breaking, building, knocking, finding
Doors closed, or slowly opening
And their mind is action dressing.

When we live as children do
We may come to read their wisdom:

Do not wear 'You should not': only
As some hide their virgin faces!
Let the sunlight touch your navel
Touch your thighs as male eyes do
Live as children do at play!

Have you seen a single painter
Who has always shut his eyes?

Look at real life as painting:
Real laughter, real weeping,
Salty, biting in the nose.
Live with monks, in hospital;
Talk to priests, to prisoners, poets,
Talk to scientists and watchmen,

[73]

Bakers, bankers, pregnant girls;
Sportsmen, hippies – Yes. And why not?

Ask the regulars at banquets
What it tastes to dine on laughter;
Lick an ice of cold refusal,
Eat a steaming dish of wonder,

Go to parliament; to a factory,
Kaufhof, Bahnhof, Friedhof, library!

Dance the waltz in silk, organza;
Dance the polka in a Maxi,
And the Soul in an air of Nothing.

Try the swings and roundabouts.
Ride a race-car at a fair,
Join a festive Carnival crowd,
Swim at Sylt, all stark and salty:
Ride a surf, a horse, a bike,
Fling a passion invitation
To a rich inclusive class
For a dance of live sensation,
Dance till dawn, in a Discotheque
Just as some go to the Louvre
Or wander round Pinckothek.

If behaviour dressed as monks
How could Modigliani paint?
How could Goethe, Shakespeare, Joyce,
Lawrence, Henry Moore and Munch
Link to free the eternal feminine

[74]

Rather be a free Lautrec
Than adore his hanged-up work.

Shadow falls away from where
A light shines upon desire;
Face the light. It's good for seeing.

He who comes must step from shadow.
Let us see him in fair light;
Darkness is for those who go.

To Our Common Experience

Master strategists, and raised
Lamps of our enlightenment,
You who shed the tears of war,
Swallowed, to avoid mass panic;

You who saw your women huddle
Into holes for warmth and shelter
When disaster shrieked above,
And snakes of anguish crowded round you,

Saw your proud youth killed in trenches,
Ground to death by moving tanks;

You who fought in burning debris
Of great houses you have loved;
Saw a storm of fire rage
Through a crowded street of Art;

Saw a fire-bomb burn a friend
To a faceless lump of grief
In a voiceless yell of pain;

You who saw the wrecks of war
Bundle what they could in blankets,
Huddle children and the aged
On to carts to flee destruction
On a hopeless, endless journey;

You who saw lame children run,
Lean, in tatters, begging bread;
Old men's legs like the sticks that helped them;
Men in rags, in queues, hungry,
In a biting winter wind;

Women weeping, falling over
Boys and children blown to bits
By a bomb that burst their hearts;

You who saw your wives barter
Jewels, watches, linen, clothes,
For potatoes, butter, meat;

Saw your manhood drained of strength
By disease and malnutrition;

Walked with bare and blistered feet
Through a winter, spiky rubble;

Saw a horde of rats scuttle
Over altars, swimming pools,
City squares, and beds for kings!

You who walked among the wounded . . .
Boys who could be scientists,
Industrial magnates, doctors, priests,
Inventors of the highest rank,
Dying in their pools of blood;

What is it you felt and swore on,
Seeing all you loved and treasured
Desecrated or destroyed;

[77]

Food for children and the sick
Flattened by a tank in squalor,
Promise, that your children were,
Cut away before their summer?

Why did all this come to you,
You who saw all this, and more?

Cast a cold eye on pride
And remember us who lift
Weapons obsolete for war
Against a ruthless enemy
Many times as crippling, killing
As the one you knew, and fought;
Deadlier, subtler, quieter.

Hear me shout about a fiercer
Total war condition on our hands,
Laying waste our youth and will,
Killing children, maiming mothers,
Robbing many of the food
And the water we require,
Poisoning, preventing growth,
Seeking allies from our habits,
Throwing the good of the intellect,
And the rigours we require
For advance into modern ways
Into scorching ignorance.

You who shared our fate, yet live,
And require no long reporting,
Nothing that we suffer, die of,
Can be shocking news for you.

Allies, safe, strong, away
From the fire and the stench,
From the mad, metallic terror
Of automatic gun, and bomb,

Like your dreams, our dreams are nightmares,
Strange noises full of madness,
More distressing, being silent,
So disarming with their sadness.

Do not say you've had enough;
For fire in a crowded city,
Or killing bombs from a darkened sky,
Have no manners, know no barriers,
Do not spare a bank, or church,
Parliament or new apartment.

And when you meet a bully pressing
A passing neighbour on the ground,
Life requires that you should feel
'It's him today, or me tomorrow',
And, with all the strength you've got,
Push that bully off you both.

At a Railway Station

Glass doors swing,
And flowers see her step outside,
She who is their smile, their seen secret,
Out on a pavement, in a crowd,
On, into shadow of a Dom.

A blonde, well formed,
Black caped, cute
In black winter boots
Covered all over, except for the back
Of her ripe, young legs,
And high, higher up her thighs . . . she
Passes; and
Men's eyes
Are butterflies
Flying over flowers
That are her clean beauty,
Sought, seen.

She knows it, and it shows
As she stirs a summer brightness
In the dull winter crowd.

But will she in tomorrow's fog
Be a yellow guiding light
On a city's busy roads?

Will she bring a summer blood
Coursing through our freezing limbs?

Or will she puncture with her nails
The plastic bag of blood we gave;
Wave it high above her head, and
Splash it with contemptuous gestures
Into eyes of innocents?

The Crooked Tree

Thirty years
grown crooked . . .
that tree!

And you say
in a day
you can let it
stretch straight?

Back Home

Back home,
The rich, in age, is prouder
As elder.

No other
Role fits his gravity; his form.

We do not come
Of age, to break the norm
In anarchy, pretending we get younger
Growing older, claiming
A right, competing
Uncouth children spitting.

Worse still, praising
Them for spitting.

Our Extensions in Time

Newly married,
New corn, young,
Live-wood, sap-flow,
Sugar-cane sweet.
Feeling fingers.
Finding eyes.

Slung across your mind's shoulders
Are collecting bags of memory.

Time greys with many days
Till your children, and their children
Climb your knees unsteadily,
Calling: 'Grand-ma
Up! and out. Out, with us
Into life of street.
Come and play. Come and play.'

And when you've seen them off to sleep,
When in peace you tidy up; sweep
To gather the day's torn beads
And keep the lanes of the spirit clear,

Only you can know it grow.
Your vital substance branching still
Across time's waste of loneliness
In the soil your children till.

A Decent Wage
(*A cry from below*)

Four pounds a month
For me,
My wife
And three
Grown children.

Four pounds
For five mouths a month.

Four pounds
Our prison bars
Behind which we can see
The city lights,
The green hills
Stretching from our door, out, away
To the happiness of wealth
In our friendly sun
From our dark cells,
Dingy, at noon.

You said I would receive
An extra two pence
Every day.
An extra two pence,
Two pence only . . .
For five angry mouths
Hungry for the happiness
Of wealth, without the means
To gain the skill to earn
Our due, at will.

While your chains kill,
Keep your two pence still.

[84]

How Say You?

Detachment prods
Our litter with its pole,
Steps gingerly along our pond
Of steaming rot.
Avoids contamination, getting wet:
And tests; inspects
Which terror, anger or distress
Is clearly well expressed.

Along the Corridor

Born too late
we have come
rather new to the scene
of joined battle
for the rights and risks of man

We walk slowly
through long corridors
passing shut doors
on either side . . .
doors leading into side rooms
of bitter bigotries
and frays under skies
dark with flying poisonous arrows

We pass murals on the doors
carved as record or as warning
Here are bundles of a broom
intact, with a single, broken thrice . . .

There, a father gives his sons
equal sticks of sugar cane
as if to say You, sons, are equal
Equal as my sons . . . my own

Here a rich man weeps
he cannot share his farm
with a rival neighbour
There a protest from the rich
that the levelling of wealth
is a smashing of success

and a boost of parasites
idolizing lazy drop-outs

But the last opening door
sums it all up
in the keeper and his brother
Aren't we all so indeed
Each his brother's keeper?

So Far

Raindrops in the sea,
When shall we be rivers, lakes,
Marking the land with our paths,
Our beds, our depths,
Our life of fish, of plants?

We've fallen as raindrops
Over seas that bore the name
Of Ghana long before the Portuguese
Came for a piece of land to build on:
Have fallen as rain, twenty centuries or more.

Time we grew into her rivers,
Bathing roots of her Odum trees
Marking her with the power we are.

Time we burst out, rose as spring
Reaching for the sky;
Gathered into lakes, cool,
Reflecting from our depths
All it takes
In size, exposure, usefulness
To give
New livelihood to the many, the deprived:
To drive
From place to far off place, conveying
Men to goods,
And goods to men, quicken trade,
Increasing food,
Increasing money's worth and bulk,
Making it a symbol of the consciousness
That is our culture,
Keeping it secure as symbol
Till its worth is understood.

Only Thorns

She who in our summer garden
Opened eyes of fervid colour
In the bright light of her loving.
To delight the world and me,
Bared breasts of the finest freshness,
Full, in folds of softest fur
In a scented bed of roses
Whose thighs rocked my midnight sleep
On high-tide moon-lit waves of joy,

After seven months of married nearness
Now has thorns for hair on eyelids,
Thorns for nipples, thorns on lips,
And her tongue is rough with thorns.

She turns in withering scorn to me,
Slashes me across my eyes,
Stings my lips in a bleeding kiss,
Stirs an ash of grey dismay
Behind her in her windy wiles,
And wonders why I shut my eyes
And walk away and feel no urge to
Hold her in a silk of pleasure
As I did before we married.

The Victim

What does he think,
This boy, so sick,
So swollen in the trunk and joints,
So much in pain . . .
What does he think?
What does he think
Of all this noise,
This dancing, fearsome fetish priest
Who waves a chicken over him
To charm away
Without success
A pain he cannot share . . .
What does he think?
What does he think,
This wretched child
Whose tongue is parched,
Whose body twitches under grip
Of passion and disease,
As filth and ignorance
(incarnate in bad fetish priests)
Runs down his throat
In sordid overdose
Of bitter herbs?
What does he think?
What can he think
But that a curse has caused the pain?

Have you no pity,
You who stand and stare,
You who know,
Or else should know
That this is piteous wickedness . . .

You scholar, clerk,
No pity, lawyer, priest
Guard of the word of God . . .
No power, scientist,
To save this wretched, dying boy
From this infernal thing,
This tyranny of foolishness,
This criminality of quacks . . .?

How long shall children
Such as this,
Endure this painful wrong?

The Gift of Fire

A fire lights itself in us at birth,
And may continue radiant or else die
According to the way we wake to life;
And he through whom new rays of light may break
Is he whose childhood fire never dies.

A living bundle and a seething wish
Is what a child in a happy nursery is:
Forever on the move, it seeks and finds,
In wonder, mirth, adventure and in tears.

Soon afterwards, wise nurture must expose
New fuel sources in and round the child
To feed its flame that it may brighter burn
Into the age of youth when work is joy.

Some guiding love must tame the seething fire,
That it may quicken life, and not consume it,
And give a brighter light for clearer sight
To make an easier search for pearls of life.

When manhood's glowing coal succeeds the blaze,
And middle age with ripe experience comes,
New loves and old may mingle in the glow
And memory call back ardours long since past,
As hearts repose in warm serenity.

The end . . . which is no end may come at last,
When what remains of the mystic childhood fire
Is a pair of fine old eyes in a wise old age,
And a heart containing love's unconquered flame . . .
The sacred flame which is a gift to man.

Dying Birth

For me, to die
Would be to go abroad, on a holiday.
And if death should come,
I'd wish I could plan ... prepare,
As I'd have done,
Looking forward to a happiness
Somewhere, on some cool sand, in the sun,
With sea-sound laden fresh wind for a friend,
Far from the town where weeping has begun.

Stale Comment

Day after day
We've stirred and warmed
Yesterday
To eat today.

Now we are fed up;
Tired of rancid
Running butter
In our hot, unsettling weather.

Who will cook a meal
For us, fresh today,
Enough, each day. . . .

A modern comment
On our life now;
Our maturities and joys. . . .

Not a fourth-hand memory
Of a stale and tasteless past?

Gun Darkness

In the darkness of the gun
It's in vain to call for sun.

Broken eyes streaming blood,
Broken skulls spurting blood,
Broken jaws, arms, bowels,
Squirting slime, dung, blood;
Broken hopes lost in howls . . .
These are the horrid rubble
In gun darkness where men stumble.

Don't Worry

My love is like a candle-light
In a night of moths.
But she is safe as an egg is safe
In a hill of ants.

To Work and Life

When wise Ananse won the bet
To take Puff Adder alive, along
To the heavenly throne of Nyankopong
As proof of his superior wit,
Divine decree proclaimed him lord
And author of the Akan lore.
And what was Nyankonsem before,
Thenceforth became Anansesem.

Next to God, came none but him.
And to him, the fish, the bird, the beast,
The tree, the river, and the sea,
And men, from greatest to the least,
Looked for justice and advice.

But though so powerful and so wise,
He seemed not always right or kind;
    His deeds were mirror of his world . . .
Its cruelties, and joys of mind,
Its marriage beds, perfected deaths,
Its horrors, toils, and honest hearts,
Its meeting lips, and withering tongues,
Its hell from which all love departs.
And all the creatures knew of this.

This puzzle was the boil that burst,
When once in all All-Creation Conference
Of living and non-living forms
With Kweku Ananse in the chair,
Tiny fishes cried for help
Against the murderous throats of whales,

And whales, in anger, fumed
Against the T.N.T. harpoon.

Next, epidemic viruses
Complained against the horrid chemists;
And the endoparasitic worms
Kicked up hell against the doctors
While their patients writhed and died.
Lambs bleated angry protests
At the lions, wolves and tigers;
And the grass, in rustling anger,
Asked protection from the lambs.

Men accused the poisonous snakes,
While they in turn, in anger, charged
Secretary birds for being heartless!
Answering human charges with . . .
'We kill neither for fear nor malice!'
The lady praying mantis blushed
While her partner told about
Post-copulation carnal feasts.

And from the centre of the earth,
Roared volcanic protests at
The crushing weight of earth and sea;
And the mountains in their turn
Cursed the hot volcanic lava
That destroys their shapes, and dress!
Hurricanes, typhoons and floods
Blamed all else for impeding traffic,
While their victims, in distress
Pointed at the killing havoc.

Deserts railed against the sun,
While the Arctic eyed the deserts.
Forest trees burnt out by lightning
Cut their nose to spite their faces.
Everyone was in revolt,
And everyone seemed justified.

Man, at war within himself,
Cursed the fact that he could dream,
Seeing visions, feeling love,
Yet failing to make feeling fact;
But knowing what it is to be
Afflicted by the fear of evil.

Suddenly, in wild despair,
Million angry voices shouted
'We don't want to kill or die
Yet we stop, only to die.
What have you to tell us, Kweku?'

'Nyankopong is over all;
Mightier far than all of us;
He can help.' 'Why doesn't He?'
'Perhaps He cannot'. 'Or He will not!'

'Either case, can He be God?
Can He be Almighty, Father?
Twedeampong, Creator-Spirit?'

So they shouted in rebellion;
And the stench that reeked from them

Was such, that the distant sun took cover
Behind a screen of pitch-black cloud.

After nodding his consent,
Kweku Ananse rose, and spoke.
'All these questions weigh on me
Just as much as they, on you.
I'll to God tomorrow morning.
Till I come, be calm and patient.
Call no strikes. The world must on.
In any case, it will go on
Whether you work, or do not work,
But carry on, till I return.
Gentle beasts, and gentle trees,
Gentle elements, and earth,
Gentle Ladies, Gentlemen
Our world-wide Conference is dissolved.'

Early on the following day
Kweku Ananse, stooping low
With his pot of boiling questions
Perched securely on a snake
Rolled into a carrying pad
On his bald and shining head,
Started on his upward journey
To the throne of Nyankopong.

There, at last, he knocked and bowed,
Putting down his load of questions
As the heavens welcomed him.
After customary drinking,
And the customary greetings,

He began his many questions.
'Tell me of the human questions!
All the rest seem pseudo-questions.'

Nyankopong thus cut him short.
'I'll begin again, then.' 'Yes'.
'First, the question of hard work.
Work . . . the pressing need to work.'
'What of it?' The heavens thundered.
'Must men work themselves to death?'

'Not to death, rather to life.
That's the law we all go by,
And I Myself laid down that law;
And I Myself enjoy My work;
Though often it may seem so pointless
To the time-bound, finite man.
Tell man this, that work is good.
Work is good for men . . . all men!'
'So is pain?' 'Yes, so is pain,
If, suffering, man masters it.'
'What of death?' 'That too is good,
Though at times 'tis hard to bear.
But it's merciful and good,
Good for men, made as they are.'
'And volcanoes, famine, evil?
Incurable disease, and crime?'
'Some of these are man's own making,
And he must accept the cost
In suffering, and senseless fear.'
'But the others, what of them?'
'Ask no more, but tell them this . . .

'I can make them what they wish . . .
Quite immune to suffering;
But they can't be, and be man.
They are men. I made them so;
Prone to suffer, hate and die.
But the promise of my work
Is that they can ask me questions
Cursing heaven for its "ills",
From the heart of the best in them,
And the best needs that, for growth;
And if the questionings are real,
I can set to work, and guide,
Educate, transform, and redeem
The final vision locked in them.
Men are my care. Go tell them that.
It is not that I can't or will not.
What appears in me a weakness
Is intentional, apparent.
And my weakness is man's chance;
His priceless chance to work with me.
My need of him in this is vital;
And though it is not absolute,
Yet I choose to work with him.
Yes, I choose to work through him.
Let him take his chance, and live,
Or complaining merely, die.

'Much of life is what it is,
Beckoning to heroism.
Men are made by what they do;
And doing is incarnate thinking.

'The lovely dahlia springs from dung,
The phoenix rises from its ashes.
Death itself gives birth to life.
'Tis the joy of sacrifice.

'Go. Ananse, tell them that.
Don't despair if they are slow
To accept what I have said.
In the end, I know they will,
And in accepting, know the joy
I strive with them to make them for;
And knowing it, discover Me . . .'

The heavens thundered. Then a silence.
And Ananse took his leave.

Back to earth, Ananse met,
Again, creation at a Conference.
And though he did not speak a word,
From his eyes that saw God's glory,
Shone the answers to their questions,
And all dispersed, to Work and Life.